the guide to owning a

Peki

Muriel Lee

The Publisher wishes to acknowledge the following owners of the dogs in this book, including: Mrs. Robert Ballinger, Mary Gay, Sandi Gibson, Gloria Henes, Erna and Herbert Holcombe, Linda Jarrett, E. Jenner, Edith Jones, Jeannine Joyal, Vernon Lorenzen, Sheila McClure, Elizabeth Nisbet, Linda Nolken, Elaine Rigden, Sylvia Roznick, Ev Spaulding, Susan Speranza, Elizabeth Tilly, DeAnn and Larry Ulmer, LuAnn Walters, Amanda West

T.F.H. Publications, Inc.
One TFH Plaza
Third and Union Avenues
Neptune City, NJ 07753

ISBN 0-7938-2203-3

Printed and bound in the United States of America

Printed and Distributed by T.F.H. Publications, Inc.
Neptune City, NJ

Contents

The Peke's unique style and good nature has earned him the admiration of dog fanciers everywhere.

Introduction

The Pekingese! The "Lion Dog!" He carries the mystique of the Orient in a small body, and what a star he makes in the canine universe! The Pekingese is a unique breed that has the most endearing of personalities and manners found among any breed.

This book will give you an overview of the breed, its history, its characteristics, and the breed standard. You will also learn about puppy care, training, and health.

Although this may not be the dog for everyone, the Pekingese is as handsome as they come, and his good nature, calmness, and companionship is hard to beat. He is small in stature but large in stamina. His heavy coat may be a challenge for some, as he will require more care than any other short-haired breed. But once a Pekingese moves into your household and takes over, you will find it hard not to lose your heart to this delightful animal, and you will remain a devotee of the breed for a lifetime.

The epitome of "a big dog in a small package," the Pekingese is a devoted and loving companion.

History of the Pekingese

The Pekingese is a centuries-old breed. Known for over 2,000 years in China, they were unknown to the western world until the mid-1800s, when the Manchu society came to an end after the royal palace was over-run by the British army. Because the dog was revered by royalty, the Peke was rarely seen outside palace walls before that time, and anyone found taking a Pekingese from the royal palace would be stoned to death. They were referred to as the "Lion Dogs" because they had massive chests and fronts with a lion-like mane. In addition, in spite of their small stature, they had the courage of a lion. Pekes were also called the "Sleeve Dog," because a small Peke could be carried in the voluminous sleeves of the royal robes.

The history of the Pekingese, originally called the Fu, dates back four centuries, according to Chinese historians. When the capital moved to Peking under the Manchus, the name was changed to the Peking Dog. Under the Manchus, the palace dogs achieved their greatest glory. For hundreds of years, the dog, through selective breeding, was bred for his small size, bowed legs, and flat face.

When the British troops marched upon the summer palace in 1860, the emperor and empress fled taking all of their possessions with them. In their haste to leave, five Pekingese were left behind, and when the British officers invaded the palace, they took these unusual dogs and returned to England with them tucked under their arms. Dorothy Quigley, authority and well-known breeder, wrote that when the English sacked the palace, they found these dogs guarding the body of their mistress who had committed suicide. Of these dogs, a parti-colored bitch called Looty was presented to Queen Victoria, one pair was given to Lord John Hay, and the other pair was presented to the Duke and Duchess of

Richmond. These five dogs were very small, weighing between five and six pounds each.

As the decades progressed, the political situation in China changed, and the Orient was opening to the Westerners who brought more of these unusual dogs back to England. By 1890, the Pekingese population in Britain had increased to a sufficient number, enabling the breed to be exhibited at a dog show. In 1893, Pekin Pete was imported by Loftus Allen, a commander of a ship doing business in the Chinese trade. He was first shown at the 1894 Chester show under the classification of Foreign Dogs. By 1895, Mrs. Allen imported Pekin Prince and Pekin Princess, two black Pekes that formed the basis of the Pekin strain.

The Duke of Richmond, recipient of two of the early Pekes, started the Goodwood Kennels, which was later taken over by Lord and Lady Algernon Lennox. For many years, Goodwood Pekingese were regarded as the best of the breed in England. In the meantime, Mrs. Douglas Murray imported two very famous dogs from China: Ah Com and Mimosa. A number of Goodwood bitches were bred to Ah Com, and the first Pekingese champion of England, Goodwood Lo, was sired by this famous stud dog. The second champion, English Peke, was a grandson of Lo, Ch. Goodwood Chun.

Because of his lion-like mane and courageous personality, the Pekingese was often referred to as the "lion dog."

The Peke's small size earned him the nickname "Sleeve dog," because a tiny Peke could easily be carried within the folds of a royal robe.

Prior to 1898, Pekingese had been shown in the Any Variety class, but in 1898, the Ladies Kennel Association offered a special class for the breed. Later in that year, the Aquarium show offered eleven classes for Pekingese; however, Pekin Pretty was the only entry.

Early English history includes many notables who either received Pekingese as gifts or purchased outstanding dogs from China. In addition to Mrs. Loftus Allen, George Brown, a Vice Consul in China, imported several well-known dogs. A pair were imported by Admiral Sir William Dowell in 1885, and in 1889, Commander Gamble gave Mrs. Browning the Peke Fantails, the foundation of the Brackley line.

This was the first kennel to produce the short-faced Pekingese in England. Chang and Lady Li were given to Major Heuston in 1898, and they became the foundation of the Grey-stones Kennel. The last of the palace dogs were imported to England in 1900.

By 1900, the Manchu, Alderbourne, and Broadoak Kennels were all active. The Alderbourne Kennel, owned by Mrs. Ashton Cross and later her daughter, Cynthia Ashton Cross, was active for 70 years, disbanding in the early 1960s.

There were many notable English champions in the early 1900s. Tsan Pam of Chinatown was the outstanding sire of his day, and if a pedigree were carried back far enough (providing one had a large enough sheet of paper), his name would appear in the background of most modern Pekes. Ch. Chu Erh from the Alderbourne Kennel was said to have style, a perfect body, and an excellent tail carriage. With his showmanship, he was a top competitor in the ring.

Oeun Teu Tang was a masculine dog that had an excellent head and large, dark eyes, a trait passed along to his offspring. Ch. Chinky Chog was a large dog with the correct coat texture, and many considered him the ideal example of the early Pekingese. He had a tremendous positive influence on the breed. Ch. Tai Yang of Newnham, owned by Mrs. Herbert Cowell, won 40 Challenge Certificates, was an ideal showman and an outstanding sire.

As the popularity of the Pekingese spread throughout England, the Japanese Spaniel Club took an interest in the breed. By 1898, they drew up the first standard for the Pekingese. The Pekingese Club was founded in 1904 to promote a small, compact dog weighing less than ten pounds.

The Pekingese arrived in the US in the early 1900s, with imports coming into the country from China as early as 1903. Although many dogs were imported directly from China, the English-bred

The Pekingese made his first appearance in the United States in the early 20th century.

Pekes made the greatest impact upon the breed in America.

The first Peke exhibited in the US was shown in the miscellaneous class at the Philadelphia show in 1901. By 1906, the American Kennel Club (AKC) recognized the breed, and classes were offered for the breed at sanctioned shows.

The first US champion was Ch. T'sang of Downshire. Ch. Chaou Ching-Ur, owned by Dr. Mary Cotton, was the first champion bitch bred by the Dowager Empress and imported to America. By 1909, the Pekingese Club of America, founded by Dr. Cotton and several other individuals, was formed, and the first specialty show was held at the Plaza Hotel in New York City. This was indeed a gala affair with an entry of 95 dogs, expensive silver trophies, and a ballroom decorated with Chinese silks and bronze Fu dogs. This was a society affair attended by social leaders including financier J. Pierpont Morgan, an early enthusiastic patron of the breed. Mr. Morgan remained a very active figure in the breed for some years, and at the time of the formation of the national club, he was listed as the honorary president.

It is interesting to note that this was not the first society-type specialty held in a New York hotel. The French Bulldog Club of America held their first specialty at the Waldorf-Astoria Hotel in New York City in 1898. The show was greeted with great interest and enthusiasm by the press, as this was the first sanctioned show of the breed. It was also the first time a specialty show of any breed had been held in such lavish surroundings. In addition, the society of New York was in attendance. The *New York Herald* reported, "Never was a bench show held within so sumptuous an environment as that of the French Bulldog held at the Waldorf-Astoria yesterday afternoon and evening. Far up in the sun parlor, on the top most floor of the building, amid palms and potted plants and rich rugs and soft divans, 50 bulldogs were on exhibition."

The Pekingese thrived, and by the 3rd National Specialty, held in 1913, the entries reached 168. Two trophies for outstanding performance were introduced: The J. P. Morgan Trophy for Best in Show and the James Gordon Bennett Trophy (president of the Pekingese Club of America) for Best in the American-Bred Classes. In 1937, both of these trophies were retired into permanent possession by two breeders. Each trophy had to be won five times for permanent possession. Mrs. Dorothy Quigley took home the Morgan Trophy, while Misses Clara and Margaretta Lowthen retired the Bennett Trophy.

By 1910, Pekingese puppies were listed for sale in show catalogs. The *New York Times* was enthusiastic in covering Pekingese events, probably with more interest in the social register owners than in the dogs themselves. Entries at the 1914 Specialty reached a phenomenal 289.

The list of kennels, winning dogs, and their owners is extensive for the first half of the century in America, but several individuals who made a major contribution to the breed should be mentioned.

Mrs. Harry Sears of Wu Kees Kennel

After moving away from the East Coast and into the rest of America, the Pekingese won the admiration and respect of many dog fanciers.

imported Eng. Am. Can. Ch. Rajah of Hesketh Wu Kees. He was a massive black and tan dog with great substance, soundness, and an abundant coat. He is described as an unforgettable Pekingese. Mr. and Mrs. Herbert Mapes of the Whitworth Kennel bred Pekes into the 1950s. Mrs. Mapes was a very talented painter and turned out exquisite portraits of the Pekingese. Mrs. Christine Hager of the Chu Chows Kennel, Mr. and Mrs. F. C. McAllister, Mr. and Mrs. Frank Downing, and Mrs. F. Y. Mathis, all Easterners, made their

mark upon the breed, either by the dogs they bred or the dogs they imported from England.

Mrs. Jane Austin of the Catawba Kennel bred Pekes for many years, with her most famous dog being Ch. Che Le of Matsons, a beautiful, compact, red, showy male. He was the first of the Pekingese to be a consistent all-breed Best in Show winner, with more than 30 wins to his credit. Austin imported the best of English stock. Her kennel manager and handler was the well-known Ruth

Burnette Sayres. Unfortunately, when Mrs. Austin died, all of her dogs were put to sleep at her request.

Sarah Hodges of the Dah Wongs Kennel was able to produce a distinct strain of Pekes by linebreeding very carefully within her kennel. They had beautiful heads and sturdy conformation. Her consistent winner was Ch. Yo Ling, specialty winner in 1939. Misses Clara and Margaretta Lowthen had over six generations of homebreds in their Clamarlow Kennel, including many champions and specialty winners. The kennel and the sisters were admired for quality and sportsmanship.

In the mid-1920s, the Dah Lyn Kennels was established by John Royce and his sister, Caroline. Their most famous dog was Ch. Kai Lo of Dah Lyn, a bitch that was a multiple all-breed Best in Show winner, in addition to winning the Toy Group nearly 50 times. Mr. Royce showed his own dogs with enjoyment, put them down to perfection, and was a wonderful supporter of the breed.

By the 1930s, the breed began to move out from the East Coast and into the rest of America. Charmaine Lansdowne moved to California from England and brought the foundation of her Cha Ming Kennel with her. She consistently produced top dogs that were well balanced, had profuse coats, and were noted for their showmanship. Muriel Freeman, in the Midwest, imported English stock and bred under the Pekeholme prefix. Mrs. Murray Brooks of Tien Hia Kennels in Texas produced winning stock. She imported Ch. Ku Chi of Caversham from England in 1949; he proved to be a great stud dog.

Mrs. Zara Smith of the Jalna Kennels in Canada and the Pacific Northwest bred Int. Ch. Wee Starlott. She was the dam of 8 champions and grandam of 15 more. Mrs. Quigley wrote that this was a magnificent bitch. Over 50 champions came out of this kennel, and it was noted that her love and support of the breed was remarkable. Mrs. Quigley wrote of Mrs. Smith, "It is hard for me to write about Jalna. I have known Zara Smith for years. I believe we have persevered more than many other old kennels to promote and keep our breed in the limelight, trying to keep it the most popular of all Toy Breeds."

The woman whose kennel made the greatest impact upon the breed was Mrs. Richard S. Quigley (Dorothy A.) of Orchard Hill Kennels. She bred and imported Pekingese from 1930 until her death in 1970. Quigley and her dogs were a formidable challenge to any other competitor in the ring. From her kennel came 150 to 200 champions. By 1950 she already had nine generations of winners in her kennel. Her dogs won 24 National Specialties between the years of 1931 and 1965, a truly remarkable feat for any kennel of any breed.

Quigley's famous dogs were many. Ch. Grey Spider of Hesketh was the first big winner that she campaigned. Ch. Jai Son Fu of Orchard Hill was considered for many years to be the finest Peke bred in the US. He was sound and well balanced, with a beautiful head, body shape, front, and rear.

He won the National Specialty six times, won the group at the Westminster Kennel Club and at the prestigious Morris and Essex shows. He was considered an outstanding dog. Ch. Bonraye Fo Yu was an all-breed Best in Show winner. Int. Ch. Pierrot of Hartlebury was her primary stud dog and produced many champions. Mrs. Quigley imported dogs when an outstanding one came along, but she was primarily interested in her homebreds. In *The Book of the Pekingese* by Anna Katherine Nicholas and Joan McDonald Brearley, there are numerous photographs of Mrs. Quigley and her beautiful dogs, all in perfect bloom, with the owner proudly smiling in every photo. Her love and support of this breed was remarkable.

The Pekingese in America was indeed lucky to have had such a strong and devoted following that supported the breed in every way. They laid a very firm foundation for the breeders who would come along in the last half of the 20th century.

Nigel Aubrey-Jones and his partner, R. William Taylor, have been very active in the Pekingese world in Canada, England, and the US. Not only were they breeders of Pekingese, but Aubrey-Jones had an excellent eye for these dogs and imported some of the finest English Pekingese to Canada. Later, the dogs were sold to top US breeders where they were campaigned to great success. Many of these dogs made major contributions to the breed through their show wins and by siring excellent stock. Ch. Chik T'sun of Caversham was imported and became the Dog of the Year in Canada in 1956. Ch. Chik T'sun was sold to Mr. and Mrs. Charles Venable in the US and was handled by Clara Alford, a top Toy handler. In 1957, 1958, and 1959, Ch. Chik T'sun was ranked the Number One Toy dog in America. During this period, he won 124 all-breed Bests in Show and 163 Group Firsts, including winning the Toy Group three times at Westminster and Best in Show at this most prestigious show in 1960.

The Pekingese is a wonderful dog that inspires lifelong devotion in those who own him.

Am. Can. Ch. Lorenzens Imperial Encore, owned by Vernon Lorenzen, steals the show.

His remarkable record includes a string of 14 consecutive Bests in Show in a record 46 days. He sired at least 20 champions. Mr. Aubrey-Jones also imported Ch. Calartha Mandarin of Jehol, sold to Vera Crofton in the US. This dog was also a multiple Best in Show winner and sired many notable offspring. Numerous Pekingese winners, sires, and dams came from the St. Aubrey Kennel, but by far the one with the largest impact upon the breed was Ch. St. Aubrey Laparata Dragon, imported in 1975.

Ed Jenner of Knolland Farms in Illinois has been active in dogs for many years. His love for Pekingese dates back to the 1960s. Jenner's early top winner was Ch. Colden Jasper O'Dene Shay, "Dragon," an English import, handled by Edna Voyles. When Nigel Aubrey-Jones discovered Dragon in London,

he knew that he had found an exceptionally exciting Pekingese. He thought the dog, even at nine months old, was "intense in quality, exciting in type, illustrious in his background and challengingly independent in his demeanor." He imported Dragon to Canada for one year and then sent him to Ed Jenner to be campaigned by Ed's handler, Luc Boileau. Dragon fulfilled everyone's hopes and not only became a top winner with over 40 all-breed Bests in Show, but a top producer of winning Pekes as well. His daughter, Ch. St. Aubrey's Dragonora of Elsdon, owned by Mrs. Anne Snelling, was Best in Show at Westminster in 1982. In addition to Dragon, Mr. Jenner also owned Ch. St. Aubrey's Bees Wing of Elsdon. Again, shown by Luc Boileau, Bees Wing had over 35 Bests in Show, was a top Toy dog, and was the winner of the Quaker Oats Award. Luc Boileau capped his handling career when he handled Jenner's Pekingese, Ch. Wendessa Crown Prince to win Best in Show in 1990 at the Westminster Kennel Club. Upon his retirement, Mr. Boileau became a very popular judge of the Hound and Toy Groups, and Mr. Jenner continues to campaign and sponsor top dogs in the variety of breeds that appeal to him. These are indeed two exceptional men who have added a great deal to the dog world through their knowledge, generosity, and personalities.

Mr. and Mrs. Robert Jackson of Fourwind Kennels in Illinois started in Pekingese as early as the 1940s. They imported Ch. Merellen Manikin, who won a Best in Show on his first time out. Shown by Loraine Heichel, he had 23 Group Firsts and sired over 20 champions. The kennel imported top stock from England in the 1970s and bred five champions from the Laparata dog. In all, about 130 champions came out of this kennel.

Mr. and Mrs. W. L. Dudley of Dud-Lee's Kennels in Iowa produced their first show dog, Ch. Zodiac Joe, shown by Clara Alford. He placed in the Toy Group and became the foundation dog of their kennel. In 1969, they purchased their great show dog, Int. Ch. Ku Chin Tom Mi, a multiple Best in Show dog, that was not only a top winner but the sire of many champions for the kennel. Other notable winners were Ch. Dud-Lee's Khi Lyn's Masterpiece and Ch. Dud-Lee's Lypton's Lysander.

Michael Hill, of Akarana Kennel in Canada, bred Am. Can. Ch. Akarana the

Aggressor, a Best in Show dog at the age of 10 months. By his early retirement, he had won 30 Groups and 10 Bests in Show in Canada. He was the top Toy in Canada in 1980 and the sire of many winning dogs.

Joan Mylchreest of Briarcourt's Kennels bred two top winners. Ch. Briarcourt's Coral Gable, winner of 25 Bests in Show and 107 Group Firsts, was a group winner at Westminster Kennel Club. Ch. Briarcourt's Excelsior, sold to Robert Jacobsen, won 12 Bests in Show and 69 Group Firsts. Ch. Briarcourt's Rule Britannia was the sire of two top dogs. He sired the 1990 Westminster Kennel Club Best in Show winner, Ch. Wendessa Crown Prince, owned by Ed Jenner, and Ch. Muhlin Rob

Ch. Prairie Breeze Boogie Woogie, owned by DeAnn and Larry Ulmer, shows that looking good comes naturally to the Pekingese.

Roy of Mehling, a multiple Best in Show winner.

Mrs. Walter Jeffords had the largest Pekingese kennel in the 1980s. She originally started in Boston Terriers and fell in love with Pekes in the 1960s. For some years, she co-owned her dogs with Michael Wolf, and between the two of them a formidable team was created. They imported many British dogs that were shown by Wolf. Wolf and the dog would become a hard team to beat. Some of Mrs. Jeffords' best-known dogs were Ch. Dagbury of Calartha, Ch. Beau of Kyratown, handled by Edna Voyles, and Ch. Quiken the Stringman, a Best in Show specialty dog. She purchased American-bred Ch. Dan Lee Dragonseed from John Brown, who had been winning in great fashion on the West Coast. On his first trip out to the East Coast, with Mr. Wolf handling, Ch. Dan Lee Dragonseed won the Toy Group at Westminster. He consequently won five consecutive Bests in Show in the east. After the partnership broke up, Mrs. Jeffords took on the kennel name Chinatown.

Ruth Painter's Panora Kennels imported and bred many champions, including Ch. Oakmere the Baron, handled by Elaine Rigden, a multiple Best in Show dog and the top-winning Peke in 1975 and 1976. Mrs. Walter Maynard imported Ch. Belknap Kalafrana Caspar, sire of more than ten champions, including Mrs. Jeffords' Shinecock, a Best in Show winner. Caspar sired Velspring Velveteena in England before Mrs. Maynard imported her to the US. She was a consistent Group and Best in Show winner and one of the top show bitches in the breed.

The Pekingese has indeed had an illustrious show career in the US in the 20th century. The 21st century should only bring about more dedicated breeders and more marvelous dogs that will continue to make history for the breed.

The regal Pekingese has enjoyed an illustrious show career in the United States.

Standard
for the
Pekingese

Each breed approved by the American Kennel Club has a standard that gives the breeder a mental picture of what a specific breed should look like. All reputable breeders strive to produce animals that will meet the requirements of the standard. In addition to having dogs that *look* like a proper Pekingese, the standard ensures that the Peke will have the personality, disposition, and intelligence that is sought for in the breed.

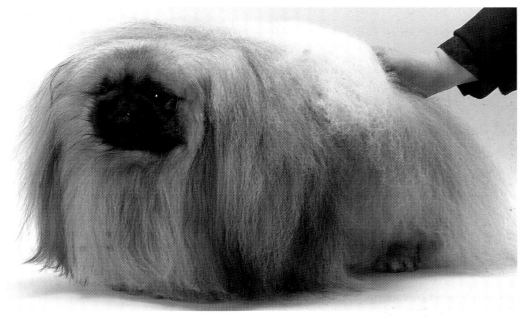

The ideal Pekingese should be well balanced and compact and should project a lion-like image of courage and boldness.

The Peke's large, dark eyes are one of his most noticeable and attractive features.

As time progressed and breeders became more aware that certain areas of the dog needed a better description or more definition, they would meet together and work out a new standard. However, standards for a breed are never changed on a whim; serious study and exchange between breeders takes place before any change is made.

THE OFFICIAL STANDARD FOR THE PEKINGESE

Revised Standard for the Pekingese

The Board of Directors of The American Kennel Club has approved the following revised standard for the Pekingese as submitted by the Pekingese Club of America, Inc.

General Appearance

The Pekingese is a well-balanced, compact dog with heavy front and lighter hind-quarters. It must suggest its Chinese origin in its directness, independence, individuality and expression. Its image is lionlike. It should imply courage, boldness and self-esteem rather than prettiness, daintiness or delicacy.

Size, Substance, Proportion

Size/Substance—The Pekingese should be surprisingly heavy when lifted. It has a stocky, muscular body. The bone of the forequarters must be very heavy in relation to the size of the dog. All weights are correct within the limit of 14 pounds, provided that type and points are not sacrificed. *Disqualification: weight over 14 pounds. Proportion*—The length of the body, from the front of the breast bone in a straight line to the buttocks, is slightly greater than the height of the withers. Overall balance is of utmost importance.

Head

Skull—The topskull is massive, broad and flat (not dome-shaped). The topskull, the high, wide cheek bones, broad lower jaw and wide chin are the structural formation of the correctly shaped face. When viewed frontally, the skull is wider than deep and contributes to the rectangular envelope-shaped appearance of the head. In profile, the Pekingese face must be flat. The chin, nose leather and brow all lie in one plane. In the natural position of the head, this plane appears vertical but slants very slightly backward from chin to forehead. *Nose*—It is black, broad, very short and in profile, contributes to the flat appearance of the face. Nostrils are open. The nose is positioned between the eyes so that a line

The Peke's coat should be long and full-bodied, but not so much that it inhibits movement or obscures the shapeliness of the body.

drawn horizontally across the top of the nose intersects the center of the eyes. *Eyes*—They are large, very dark, round, lustrous and set wide apart. The look is bold, not bulging. The eye rims are black and the white of the eye does not show when the dog is looking straight ahead. *Wrinkle*—It effectively separates the upper and lower areas of the face. The appearance is of a hair covered fold of skin, extending from one cheek, over the bridge of the nose in a wide inverted "V", to the other cheek. It is NEVER so prominent or heavy as to crowd the facial features nor to obscure a large portion of the eyes or the nose from view. *Stop*—It is deep. The bridge of the nose is completely obscured from view by hair and/or the over-nose wrinkle. *Muzzle*—

This is very short and broad with high, wide cheek bones. The color of the skin is black. Whiskers add to the Oriental expression. *Mouth*—The lower jaw is slightly undershot. The lips meet on a level plane and neither teeth nor tongue

The coat of the Pekingese may consist of a number of colors and markings, including parti-color.

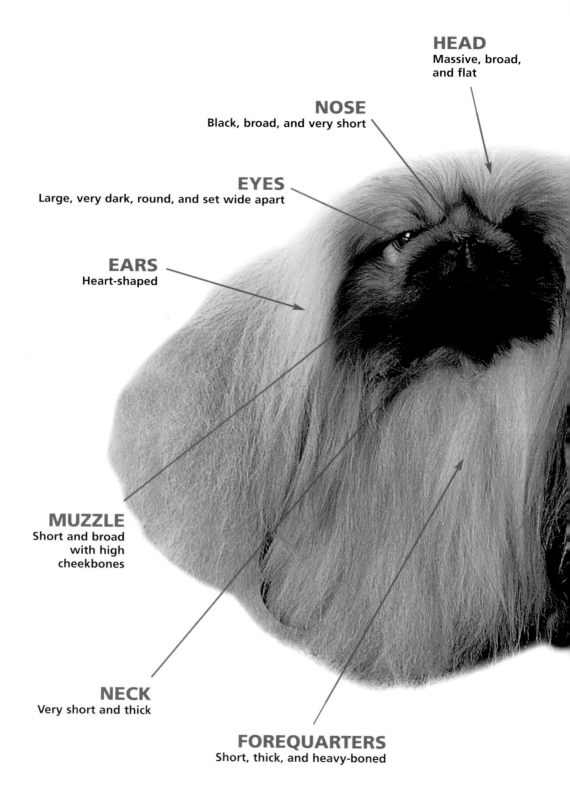

HEAD
Massive, broad, and flat

NOSE
Black, broad, and very short

EYES
Large, very dark, round, and set wide apart

EARS
Heart-shaped

MUZZLE
Short and broad with high cheekbones

NECK
Very short and thick

FOREQUARTERS
Short, thick, and heavy-boned

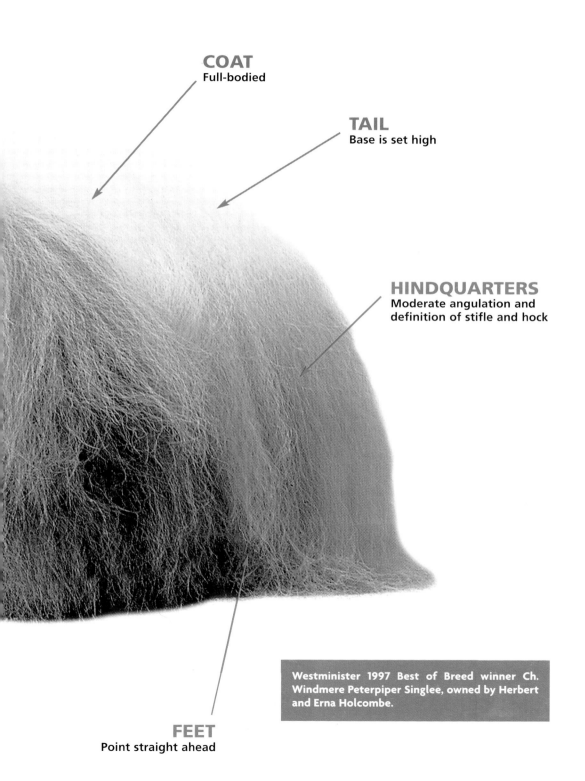

COAT
Full-bodied

TAIL
Base is set high

HINDQUARTERS
Moderate angulation and
definition of stifle and hock

Westminister 1997 Best of Breed winner Ch.
Windmere Peterpiper Singlee, owned by Herbert
and Erna Holcombe.

FEET
Point straight ahead

Although the Peke is a small dog, what he lacks in size he makes up for in personality.

show when the mouth is closed. The lower jaw is strong, wide, firm and straight across at the chin. An excessively strong chin is as undesirable as a weak one. *Ears*—They are heart-shaped and set on the front corners of the skull extending the line of the topskull. Correctly placed ears frame the sides of the face and with their heavy feathering create an illusion of additional width of the head. *Pigment*—The skin of the nose, lips and eye rims is black on all colors.

Neck, Body, Tail

Neck—It is very short, thick and set back into the shoulder. *Body*—This is pear-shaped and compact. It is heavy in front with well-sprung ribs slung between the forelegs. The broad chest, with little or no protruding breast bone, tapers to lighter loins with a distinct waist. The topline is level. *Tail*—The base is set high; the remainder is carried well over the center of the back. Long, profuse straight feathering may fall to either side.

Forequarters

They are short, thick and heavy-boned. The bones of the forelegs are slightly bowed between the pastern and elbow. Shoulders are gently laid back and fit smoothly into the body. The elbows are always close to the body. Front feet are large, flat and turned slightly out. The dog must stand well up on feet.

Hindquarters

They are lighter in bone than the forequarters. There is moderate angulation and definition of stifle and hock. When viewed from behind, the rear legs are reasonably close and parallel and the feet point straight ahead.

Soundness is essential in both forequarters and hindquarters.

Coat

Body Coat—It is full-bodied, with long, coarse textured, straight, stand-off coat and thick, softer undercoat. The coat forms a noticeable mane on the neck and shoulder area with the coat on the remainder of the body somewhat shorter in length. A long and profuse coat is desirable proving that it does not obscure the shapeliness of the body, nor sacrifice the correct coat texture. *Feathering*—Long feathering is found on the back of the thighs and forelegs, and on the ears, tail and toes. The feathering is left on the toes but should not be so long as to prevent free movement.

Color

All coat colors and markings, including parti-colors, are allowable and of equal merit.

Gait

The gait is unhurried and dignified, with a slight roll over the shoulders. The rolling gait is caused by the bowed front legs and heavier, wider forequarters pivoting on the tapered waist and the lighter, straight parallel hindquarters. The rolling motion is smooth and effortless and is as free as possible from bouncing, prancing or jarring.

Temperament

A combination of regal dignity, self-importance, self-confidence and exasperating stubbornness make for a good natured, lively and affectionate companion to those who have earned it respect.

The foregoing is a description of the ideal Pekingese. Any deviation should be penalized in direct proportion to the extent of that deviation.

FAULTS TO BE NOTED

- Dudley, Liver or Grey Nose
- Light Brown, Yellow or Blue Eyes
- Protruding Tongue or Teeth
- Overshot Upper Jaw
- Wry Mouth
- Ears Set Much Too High, Low or Back
- Roach or Swayback
- Straight-Boned Forelegs

Pekes make wonderful playmates for gentle, easygoing children, provided they are taught to obey all members of the household.

Points:

Expression 5
Nose 5
Stop 5
Muzzle 5
Legs and Feet .15
Tail 5
Skull 10
Eyes 5
Ears 5
Shape of Body .20
Coat, Feather and Condition 10
Action 10
                    Total 100

Disqualification: weight over 14 pounds.
Approved: June 13, 1995
Effective: July 31, 1995

Characteristics of the Pekingese

Of all the breeds of dog, the Pekingese is not only one of the oldest, but also one of the most elegant. Centuries of Chinese background show both in his eyes and his bearing. He knows that he was bred to be special and that he was king among the animals, as far as the royal family was concerned. This is a companion dog and, like the French Bulldog, he has been bred to be a companion. Unlike the terrier that routs out vermin or the sporting dog that flushes birds, the Pekingese has been bred

Considered one of the most elegant and regal breeds of dog, the Pekingese has been bred to be a companion that is happiest at the feet of his master or mistress.

The Pekingese has a number of unique qualities that make him a versatile and amiable breed.

Whether he lives in a city apartment or on a country farm, the Peke easily adapts to any setting, provided he is with a loving and caring family.

for centuries to keep his mistress or master company.

The Toy breeds, of which the Peke is one, are bred to be loyal, affectionate, healthy, and pleasing to look at. However, just because this breed is small in structure does not mean that it spends all of its time sitting on a lap or possibly up a sleeve if small enough. The Peke has a lot of energy but barks very little and is, in general, a quiet companion.

This is a dog that is somewhat defiant and stubborn, very confident, bold, independent, and plucky. Like a Scottish Terrier, he is often called a big dog in a small package. He will not pick a fight but is fearless and will stand his ground when pushed. He will hold up his end in an argument and will be as "bold as a lion."

Because of his small size and quiet demeanor, he can make an excellent pet in either the city or the country. He does not require a lot of exercise but will enjoy a good romp when outside.

In his *Dog Encyclopedia*, Will Judy wrote, "His pushed in nose is only the better to smell you. Give him a lorgnette and he is a perfect haughty dowager. Perhaps you say, 'I'd never own one of those dogs!' A Peke grows on you and you will like him against your will. Own one for thirty days and you won't know whether you or the Peke is smarter or saucier. He is mischievous and he seeks to taunt you on every occasion. He wants his own way in almost everything. The large, prominent, moist eyes so soulful, should be sympathetic and kind; in them they hold all the silent mystery of China; yet they only conceal a spirit of defiance, fortified by a brave heart and a daring entirely out of proportion to the size of the body which houses it."

To sum up the character of the Pekingese, the Dowager Empress Tzu Hsi wrote a poem, which formed some of the basis for an early breed standard. It said in part, "Let it be lively that it may afford entertainment by it gambol; let it be timid that it may not involve itself in danger; let it be domestic in habits that it may live in amity with other beasts..."

Purchasing Your Pekingese

When purchasing your Pekingese, be careful to buy your dog from a reputable breeder. Ask to see the dam (and sire, if on the premises), and inquire if the breeder belongs to the local all-breed kennel club and/or the Pekingese Club of America.

Although the Pekingese is within the top 30 breeds in popularity, you probably will not be able to run out and find just the dog you want when you want it. Be prepared to wait for your puppy once you have determined that

Meeting the sire and dam of the puppy you are considering will give you a good idea of what he will look and act like as an adult.

Adding a dog to your family is a lifelong commitment. Before making a decision, research the Pekingese to ensure that it's the right breed for your lifestyle.

this is the breed for you. You may have to wait six or eight months, and you may have to travel a little distance to find the right dog. Take your time. When you buy a car, you may keep it three years and then trade it in for a new model. When buying a puppy, you are making a commitment that can last anywhere from 10 to 15 years. Be sure you know what you are buying and be sure to get what you want.

If there is a regional Pekingese Club in your area or state, contact a club member for assistance in finding a puppy. Members of the Pekingese Club are there to help newcomers to the breed. They want to make certain that this is the breed for you and that you will make a good Pekingese owner. On occasion, there may be an older dog that, for one reason or another, needs a home. Give this consideration, as an older dog can be a joy to bring into the household.

Remember what the standard says, "The Pekingese is a well-balanced, compact dog with heavy front and lighter hindquarters. I must suggest its Chinese origin in its directness, inde-pendence, individuality and ex-pression. Its image in lionlike. It should imply courage, boldness and self-esteem rather than prettiness, daintiness or delicacy."

DOCUMENTS

Now, a little paperwork is in order. When you purchase a purebred Pekingese puppy, you should receive a transfer of ownership, registration material, and other "papers" (a list of the immunization shots, if any, the puppy may have been given; a note on whether or not the puppy has been wormed; a diet and feeding schedule to which the puppy is accustomed) and

Although Peke puppies are adorable and often hard to resist, they may not be the best choice for some people. Carefully consider whether a puppy or adult Peke is right for you.

When you purchase a purebred puppy, the breeder should supply you with three important documents: a health record containing an inoculation list, a copy of the dog's pedigree, and the registration certificate.

you are welcomed as a fellow owner to a long, pleasant association with a most lovable pet and more (news)paper work.

GENERAL PREPARATION

You have chosen to own a particular Pekingese puppy. You have chosen it very carefully over all other breeds and all other puppies. So before you ever get that Pekingese puppy home, you will have prepared for his arrival by reading everything you can get your hands on having to do with the management of Pekingeses and puppies. True, you will run into many conflicting opinions, but at least you will not be starting "blind." Read, study, digest. Talk over your plans with your veterinarian, other "Pekingese people," and the seller of your Pekingese puppy.

When you get your Pekingese puppy, you will find that your reading and study are far from finished. You've just scratched the surface in your plan to provide the greatest possible comfort and health for your Pekingese, and, by the same token, you do want to assure yourself of the greatest possible enjoyment of this wonderful creature. You must be ready for this puppy mentally as well as in the physical requirements.

TRANSPORTATION

If you take the puppy home by car, protect him from drafts, particularly in cold weather. Wrapped in a towel and carried in the arms or lap of a passenger, the Pekingese puppy will usually make the trip without mishap. If the pup starts to drool and to squirm, stop the car for a few minutes. Have newspapers handy in case of carsickness. A covered carton lined with newspapers provides protection for puppy and car, if you are driving alone. Avoid excitement and unnecessary handling of the puppy on arrival. A Pekingese puppy is a very small "package" to be making a complete change of surroundings and company, and he needs frequent rest and refreshment to renew his vitality.

Caring for a dog is a lifelong commitment, so make sure that the decision to bring a Peke home is a carefully considered one.

Riding in the car can be a strange and fearful experience for a puppy. The crate will provide your Pekingese with a safe place to relax while traveling.

THE FIRST DAY AND NIGHT

When your Pekingese puppy arrives in your home, put him down on the floor and don't pick him up again, except when it is absolutely necessary. He is a dog, a real dog, and must not be lugged around like a rag doll. Handle him as little as possible, and permit no one to pick him up and baby him. To repeat, *put your Pekingese puppy on the floor or the ground and let him stay there except when it may be necessary to do otherwise.*

Quite possibly your Pekingese puppy will be afraid for a while in his new surroundings without his mother and littermates. Comfort him and reassure him, but don't console him. Don't give him the "oh-you-poor-itsy-bitsy-puppy" treatment. Be calm, friendly, and reassuring. Encourage him to walk around and sniff over his new home. If it's dark, put on the lights. Let him roam for a few minutes while you and everyone else concerned sit quietly or go about your routine business. Let the puppy come back to you.

Playmates may cause an immediate problem if the new Pekingese puppy is to

Make sure that you take your Pekingese outside to relieve himself after eating, sleeping, and playing. Praise and positive reinforcement are important parts of the housetraining process.

be greeted by children or other pets. If not, you can skip this subject. The natural affinity between puppies and children calls for some supervision until a live-and-let-live relationship is established. This applies particularly to a Christmas puppy, when there is more excitement than usual and more chance for a puppy to swallow something upsetting. It is a better plan to welcome the puppy several days before or after the holiday week. Like a baby, your Pekingese puppy needs much rest and should not be handled excessively. Once a child realizes that a puppy has "feelings" similar to his own, and can readily be hurt or injured, the opportunities for play and responsibilities provide exercise and training for both.

For his first night with you, he should be put where he is to sleep every night—say in the kitchen, since its floor can usually be easily cleaned. Let him explore the kitchen to his heart's content; close doors to confine him there. Prepare his food and feed him lightly the first night. Give him a pan with some water in it—not a lot, since most puppies will try to drink the whole pan dry. Give him an old coat or shirt to lie on. Since a coat or shirt will be strong in human scent, he will pick it out to lie on, thus furthering his feeling of security in the room where he has just been fed.

HOUSETRAINING HELPS

Now, sooner or later—mostly sooner—your new Pekingese puppy is going to "puddle" on the floor. First take a newspaper and lay it on the puddle until

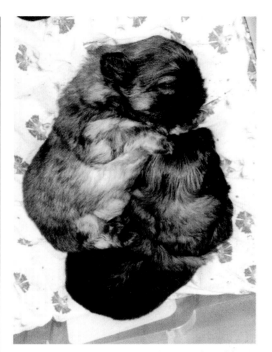

Help make your Peke's arrival as comfortable as possible by providing him with a quiet environment and soothing reassurance.

the urine is soaked up onto the paper. Save this paper. Now take a cloth with soap and water, wipe up the floor and dry it well. Then take the wet paper and place it on a fairly large square of newspapers in a convenient corner. When cleaning up, always keep a piece of wet paper on top of the others. Every time he wants to "squat," he will seek out this spot and use the papers. (This routine is rarely necessary for more than three days.) Now leave your Pekingese puppy for the night. Quite probably he will cry and howl a bit; some are more stubborn than others on this matter. But let him stay alone for the night. This may seem harsh treatment, but it is the best procedure in the long run. Just let him cry; he will weary of it sooner or later.

Feeding Your Pekingese

Now let's talk about feeding your Pekingese, a subject so simple that it's amazing there is so much nonsense and misunderstanding about it. Is it expensive to feed a Pekingese? No, it is not! You can feed your Pekingese economically and keep him in perfect shape the year round, or you can feed him expensively. He'll thrive either way, and let's see why this is true.

First of all, remember that a Pekingese is a dog. Dogs do not have a high degree of selectivity in their food, and unless you spoil them with great variety (and

A balanced diet that includes the proper amount of protein, fats, and carbohydrates will ensure that your Pekingese receives all of the proper nutrients necessary for healthy growth.

possibly turn them into poor, "picky" eaters) they will eat almost anything to which they become accustomed. Many dogs flatly refuse to eat nice, fresh beef. They pick around it and eat everything else. But meat—bah! Why? They aren't accustomed to it! They'd eat rabbit fast enough, but they refuse beef because they aren't used to it.

VARIETY NOT NECESSARY

A good general rule of thumb is to forget all human preferences and don't give a thought to variety. Choose the right diet for your Pekingese and feed it to him day after day, year after year, winter and summer. But what is the right diet?

Hundreds of thousands of dollars have been spent in canine nutrition research. The results are pretty conclusive, so you needn't go into a lot of experimenting with trials of this and that every other week. Research has proven just what your dog needs to eat and to keep healthy.

DOG FOOD

There are almost as many right diets as there are dog experts, but the basic diet most often recommended is one that consists of a dry food, either meal or kibble form. There are several of excellent quality, manufactured by reliable companies, research tested, and nationally advertised. They are inexpensive, highly satisfactory, and easily available in stores everywhere in containers of 5 to 50 pounds. Larger amounts cost less per pound, usually.

Establishing a feeding schedule with set amounts of food will help you to monitor your Peke's overall health.

If you have a choice of brands, it is usually safer to choose the better known one; but even so, carefully read the analysis on the package. Do not choose any food in which the protein level is less than 25 percent, and be sure that this protein comes from both animal and vegetable sources. The good dog foods have meat meal, fish meal, liver, and such, plus protein from alfalfa and soy beans, as well as some dried-milk product. Note the vitamin content carefully. See that they are all there in good proportions, and be especially certain that the food contains properly high levels of vitamins A and D, two of the most perishable and important ones. Note the B-complex level, but don't worry about carbohydrate and mineral levels. These substances are plentiful and cheap and not likely to be lacking in a good brand.

You can determine the effectiveness of your Pekingese's diet by looking at his appearance. He should be well covered with flesh and show good bone and muscle development.

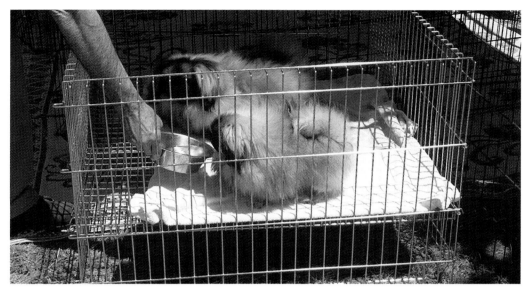

Water is an essential part of your Peke's diet. Provide him with a constant supply of clean, fresh water.

The advice given for how to choose a dry food also applies to moist or canned types of dog foods, if you decide to feed one of these.

Having chosen a really good food, feed it to your Pekingese as the manufacturer directs. And once you've started, stick to it. Never change if you can possibly help it. A switch from one meal or kibble-type food can usually be made without too much upset; however, a change will almost invariably give you (and your Pekingese) some trouble.

WHEN SUPPLEMENTS ARE NEEDED

Now what about supplements of various kinds, mineral and vitamin, or the various oils? They are all okay to add to your Pekingese's food. However, if you are feeding your Pekingese a correct diet, and this is easy to do, no supplements are necessary unless your Pekingese has been improperly fed, has been sick, or is having

puppies. Vitamins and minerals are naturally present in all the foods, and to ensure against any loss through processing, they are added in concentrated form to the dog food you use. Except on the advice of your veterinarian, added amounts of vitamins can prove harmful to your Pekingese. The same risk goes with minerals.

FEEDING SCHEDULE

When and how much food to give your Pekingese? Most dogs do better if fed two or three smaller meals per day—this is not only better but vital to larger and deep-chested dogs. As to how to prepare the food and how much to give, it is generally best to follow the directions on the food package. Your own Pekingese may want a little more or a little less.

Fresh, cool water should always be available to your Pekingese. This is important to good health throughout his lifetime.

Grooming Your Pekingese

It is important to understand that when you purchase a dog you have the responsibility of maintaining him. Think of the dog in terms of your child—you bathe your youngster, comb his hair, and put a clean set of clothes on him. The end product is a child that smells good, looks nice, and that you enjoy having in your company. It is the same with your dog—keep the dog brushed and clean and you will find it a pleasure to be in his company. Owners of Pekingese must bear in mind that they have a heavy-coated breed and that grooming is required on at least a weekly basis. Do not purchase a Pekingese if you are not willing to make this commitment.

Grooming will primarily consist of a weekly "go-over."

These are the tools that you will need to groom your dog:

Spray your Peke's coat with an atomizer to make it slightly damp before you begin to brush.

A grooming table will assist you in caring for your Pekingese. This Peke shows off his handsome coat.

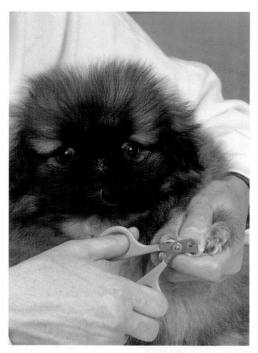

Trimming your Pekingese's nails once a week will keep them short and help get him used to grooming procedures.

- A grooming table—something sturdy with a towel to cover the top to lay your dog upon;
- A bristle brush;
- A wide-tooth comb;
- A toenail trimmer;
- A spray atomizer;
- A good pair of scissors;
- Cotton swabs;
- Old washcloths;
- Baby powder;
- A coat dressing.

If you start grooming your puppy at an early age, he will quickly learn that this can be a pleasant experience and cooperate with you. If you rarely groom him and he becomes matted, it will be an unpleasant experience for both of you.

To start, brush him for perhaps only five

Regularly check your Peke's ears for any waxy build-up. Be extremely careful around this sensitive area to avoid causing ear damage.

Begin grooming your dog at an early age—it will help him become accustomed to the weekly procedure.

Regular grooming sessions combined with an all-over body check will help you to stay on top of your Peke's physical condition while allowing you to maintain his appearance.

minutes at a time. Repeat this process daily for the first few weeks or so, lengthening the time for each grooming session. Once the pup is used to laying on the table for you and used to the brush, you should be well on your way to satisfactory grooming sessions. When showing your Peke puppy, you will bathe him often. If you are planning to campaign him in the show ring as a Special, you will probably give him only a partial bath to clean his undersides and skirts.

Before you start grooming, dampen a washcloth in warm water and rub it over the entire coat to remove any dirt particles. While doing this, wash around his eyes and the folds in his face. Baby powder should be massaged into any mats to make it easier to untangle them with either your finger or the end of a comb. The dog's ears should be checked for any wax accumulation and carefully cleaned out

with a cotton swab. Groom both the inside and outside of the ear and remove any mats. To finish off the dog's head, you may want to trim the whiskers. Some feel that trimmed whiskers give the dog an appearance of neatness.

When grooming the dog's body, start by spraying it with an atomizer to make the dog's coat slightly damp. Take the brush and brush thoroughly from the shoulders forward to the head. Continue to brush toward the head as you go down the back. At some point, you will have to lay your dog on his back in order to groom the stomach area. If your dog is not a show dog, you may want to trim some hair away from the penis or vulva in order to keep your dog clean. The dog's tail should be brushed toward the head and parted in the middle. Be sure to comb out the dog's legs and make certain that they are free of mats.

If you are considering showing your dog, you will need to have someone, preferably your breeder, show you the finer points of show grooming that will be necessary in order to have a winning Peke. If you have a busy life or are not interested in grooming, you must take your dog to a professional groomer. If this is the route you choose, plan to take your dog in at least once a month, if not more often.

Remember, you selected a Pekingese because of his beautiful coat and appearance. Leaving your dog untouched for a month or more will leave you with a matted, and perhaps, dirty dog. Your dog will be unhappy and you will be, too!

Working with Your Pekingese

Every Pekingese should be able to lie around the house, have a good meal, receive love and attention, and be taken for a walk or a romp every day. However, some owners like the challenge of working with their dog, training him to

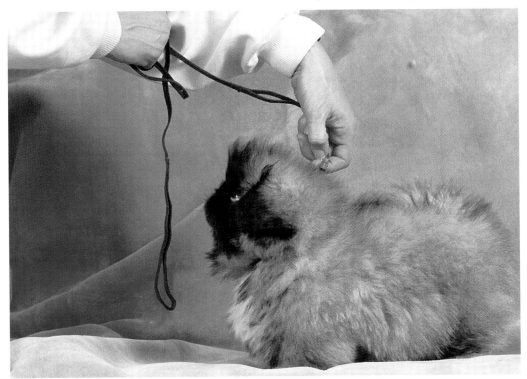

Give your Peke time to get used to the feel of a leash and collar. Once he feels comfortable, you can go anywhere together without worrying that he'll wander off.

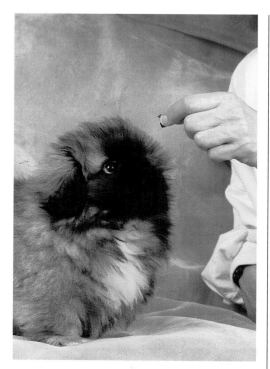

Remember to praise your Pekingese for a job well done. Always have a treat ready to let your pet know that his good behavior is appreciated.

every day, even if it is only for five minutes or so. The handler must also have patience, and the dog must have some desire to perform and willingness to please. Once this match is made, a handler and his dog can be well on their way toward an obedience degree. The handler will feel a tremendous amount of achievement and accomplishment to have such a smart little dog working by his side. Spectators at a dog show love to watch the obedience rings because they can understand what the dog is doing (or not doing) much better than when they watch the conformation rings.

follow commands, and seeing him perform. Although you do not often see Pekingese in the obedience ring, there have been Pekes that have performed very well in this activity.

Pekingese, like the Scottish Terriers, are stubborn and intelligent dogs and will be a challenge for their trainer. Obedience work is easier for those dogs that like to please—Goldens, Labradors, Poodles. However, if this is an area that you are interested in, you should take your Peke to a local obedience class. You may want to check out several different classes in your area and see which method of training appeals to you.

For obedience work, dog and handler need aptitude and determination. The handler must take time to work his dog

The time invested in training will benefit both dog and owner for a lifetime. This Peke shows off what he has learned.

Teaching your Peke good manners and obedience skills will ensure that he will become a treasured member of the family for years to come.

The Peke's affectionate and gentle nature makes him a wonderful candidate for any activity, whether it is hanging out with his friends or providing companionship to the elderly.

Obedience classes are offered throughout the country, and unless you live in a very remote area, your town or city should offer you a selection of training clubs. Even if you are not interested in pursuing obedience for a degree, you will find it worthwhile to take your puppy to the beginning classes, which usually consist of six weeks of training. During this period your dog will learn to come, sit, and heel on command. And like your child, you will find it well worthwhile to have a dog that knows his manners!

If you like to volunteer, it is wonderful if you can take your Peke to a nursing home once a week for several hours. The elderly community loves to have a dog to visit, and often your dog will bring a bit of companionship to someone who is either lonely or may be somewhat detached from the world. You will not only be bringing happiness to someone else, but you will be keeping your little dog busy—and we haven't even mentioned the fact that they have discovered that volunteering helps to increase your longevity!

Showing Your Pekingese

Dog shows have been in existence in America for well over 100 years. The Westminster Kennel Club dog show, held every year in the beginning of February in New York City, is the second oldest annual sporting event in the country, with only the Kentucky Derby having greater longevity.

If you are new to the show ring, attend a few local shows without your dog to see what the game is about. If you are competitive, have the time and money to

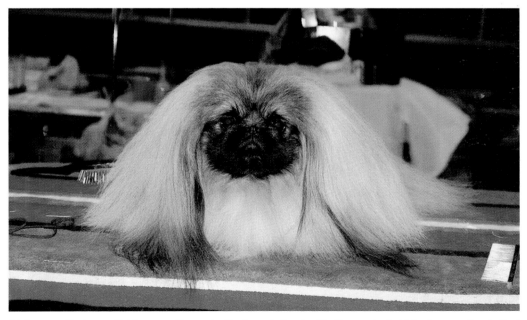

Make sure that your Pekingese adheres to the breed standard before entering him in a conformation show.

Successful showing requires dedication and hard work, but most of all, it should be enjoyable for both the dog and his handler. Shown here is Ch. Coughton Sungable of Perryaire, owned by Elaine Rigden and Amanda West.

compete, and of course, have a good dog, this may be the sport and hobby for you.

Contact your local all-breed club and find out if they offer conformation classes where you can learn how to handle your dog in the ring. Start attending these classes on a regular basis. One class does not an expert make! Your all-breed club will hold one or two matches a year and you should plan to attend these matches. Match shows are run like a dog show, but they are casual and a good place for the beginner to

learn. You will not receive any points toward a championship, but you will find out how a dog show is run, and you will learn what will be expected of you and your dog. Entry fees are minimal. This is also a good opportunity to meet the people in the breed.

When you think you are ready—your dog can walk on a lead and you feel a tiny bit of confidence—enter an AKC-licensed dog show. Remember, participating successfully in dog shows requires patience, time, money, skill, and talent. It

Even if you don't plan to show your Pekingese, he will benefit from the training and discipline you provide him.

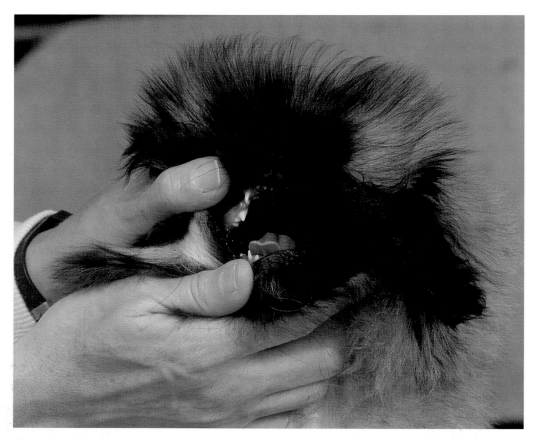

If you are going to enter your dog in conformation showing, he must be comfortable with being handled by strangers.

is the only sport where the amateur and the professional compete on an equal footing. The average dog show competitor remains active for only four to five years. Personal commitments such as children, work, and other hobbies can be a problem to those who want to compete every weekend. More often, the competitor who does not win enough will find his interest in the sport waning. A poorly groomed dog, a poorly bred dog, a dog that does not like to show, and a handler who will not take the time to handle well are all deterrents to a long stay in the sport of dog showing.

Your Healthy Pekingese

The Pekingese is one of the brachycephalic breeds. These are the flat-faced, short-nosed dogs that include the French Bulldog, Bulldog, Pug, Boxer, and Boston Terrier. These breeds have abnormally small openings to the nostrils and relatively long palates. Dogs prefer to breathe through their noses, and for these breeds it

As a responsible Pekingese owner, you should have a basic understanding of the medical problems that affect the breed.

Your Pekingese will be a valued member of the family for a long time, so you'll want to ensure that he enjoys good health and a quality lifestyle.

becomes difficult for them due to the small nasal opening. Thus, the brachycephalic breeds must increase their respiratory effort even when at rest.

In addition, the Pekingese is also an achondroplastic breed, which means that they are dwarfs, characterized by the shortening of the limbs. When the bones that arise from the growth plates are affected by achondroplasia, they will fail to develop properly, resulting in dwarfism. This is commonly found in the Dachshund as well as the Peke. In some breeds, this will be a genetic defect and bred out, whereas in the Peke it is a part of the breed and acceptable.

Because of their breathing problems, Pekingese can be very susceptible to heat and cold. Caution must be taken with this breed, particularly in the summer months. Your Peke must never be given strenuous activity in the heat and must not be out in the cold any longer than necessary. Abnormal noise, such as snorting and snoring, are also very common with this breed. As a Peke owner, you will become very familiar with and used to the snort and snores, even if your friends find it a bit humorous.

Premature degeneration of the defective discs can be a problem in the Pekingese. Symptoms are a protruding or stiff neck, lameness in either front or rear legs, and loss of bladder control. You must see your veterinarian if the condition arises. Treatment will be either anti-inflammatory drugs or surgery.

Uterine problems, such as pyometra and metritis can occur in unspayed females. Natural births in the breed are uncommon due to the large head, large shoulders, and small pelvis, and a cesarean section will almost always be called for.

Juvenile cataracts can also be a problem. An inherited disorder, you should ask your breeder if she has this problem in her line. All reputable breeders have their Peke puppies screened for eye problems.

Cancer diagnosis can occur in any breed of dog, and Pekingese are no exception. As in man, there is not always a cure, and early detection is your best form of prevention. Check your dog over for any lumps or bumps that you have not noticed before each time you groom him. Fast-growing lumps are cause for concern, particularly when found around the mammary glands. Your veterinarian should check any lump that you do not like the look of or that is growing rapidly.

Because of the breed's breathing problems, be careful not to let your Pekingese engage in strenuous activity in the heat or stay out in the cold weather for an extended period of time.

Check your Pekingese for any lumps or abrasions during his regular grooming sessions.

For problems with your Peke, you must have a good veterinarian who is familiar with the breed and familiar with your dog. Also, always purchase your Pekingese from a reputable breeder and ask her about these problems. If she has been breeding for some years she will have done her best to breed these problems out of her line. And if you wonder what a "reputable" breeder is, ask if she belongs to the Pekingese Club of America or to a local all-breed club. Also ask if she will assist you with grooming when you need help, and most importantly, if she will show you the dam of your pup.

Although this list of problems may seem long, do not be dismayed. All dogs have some kind of health or genetic problems. The very positive aspect of the Pekingese is that he is a basically very healthy and hardy dog. His life span is often 13 years or longer.

VACCINATIONS

Every puppy, purebred or mixed breed, should be vaccinated against the major canine diseases. These are distemper, leptospirosis, hepatitis, and canine parvovirus. Your puppy may have received a temporary vaccination against distemper before you purchased him, but ask the breeder to be sure.

The age at which vaccinations are given can vary, but will usually be when the pup

By using only the best quality dogs, breeders ensure that good temperament is passed down from generation to generation.

is 8 to 12 weeks old. By this time, any protection given to the pup by antibodies received from its mother via her initial milk feeds will be losing their strength.

The puppy's immune system works on the basis that the white blood cells engulf and render harmless attacking bacteria. However, they must first recognize a potential enemy.

Vaccines are either dead bacteria or they are live, but in very small doses. Either type prompts the pup's defense system to attack them. When a large attack then comes (if it does), the immune system recognizes it and massive numbers of lymphocytes (white blood corpuscles) are mobilized to counter the attack. However, the ability of the cells to recognize these dangerous viruses can diminish over a period of time. It is therefore useful to provide annual reminders about the nature of the enemy. This is done by means of booster injections that keep the immune system on its alert. Immunization is not 100-percent guaranteed successful, but is very close to this. Certainly it is better than giving the puppy no protection.

Dogs are subject to other viral attacks, and if these are of a high-risk factor in your area, then your vet will suggest you have the puppy vaccinated against these as well.

Your puppy or dog should also be vaccinated against the deadly rabies virus. In fact, in many places it is illegal for your dog not to be vaccinated. This is to protect your dog, your family, and the rest of the animal population from this deadly virus that infects the nervous system and causes dementia and death.

FIGHTING FLEAS

Fleas are very mobile and may be red, black, or brown in color. The adults suck the blood of the host, while the larvae feed on the feces of the adults, which is rich in blood. Flea "dirt" may be seen on the pup as very tiny clusters of blackish specks that look like freshly ground pepper. The eggs of fleas may be laid on the puppy, though they are more commonly laid off the host in a favorable place, such as the bedding. They normally hatch in 4 to 21 days, depending on the temperature, but they can survive for up to 18 months if temperature conditions are not favorable. The larvae are maggot-like and molt a couple of times before forming a pupae, which can survive long periods until the temperature, or the vibration of a nearby host, causes them to emerge and jump on a host.

There are a number of effective treatments available, and you should

The cat flea is the most common flea of dogs. It starts feeding soon after it make contact with the dog.

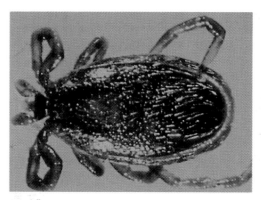

The deer tick is the most common carrier of Lyme disease. Photo courtesy of Virbac Laboratories, Inc., Fort Worth, Texas.

discuss them with your veterinarian, then follow all instructions for the one you choose. Any treatment will involve a product for your puppy or dog and one for the environment, and will require diligence on your part to treat all areas and thoroughly clean your home and yard until the infestation is eradicated.

THE TROUBLE WITH TICKS

Ticks are arthropods of the spider family, which means they have eight legs (though the larvae have six). They bury their headparts into the host and gorge on its blood. They are easily seen as small grain-like creatures sticking out from the skin. They are often picked up when dogs play in fields, but may also arrive in your yard via wild animals—even birds—or stray cats and dogs. Some ticks are species-specific, others are more adaptable and will host on many species.

The most troublesome type of tick is the deer tick, which spreads the deadly Lyme disease that can cripple a dog (or a person). Deer ticks are tiny and very hard to detect.

Often, by the time they're big enough to notice, they've been feeding on the dog for a few days—long enough to do their damage. Lyme disease was named for the area of the United States in which it was first detected—Lyme, Connecticut—but has now been diagnosed in almost all parts of the US. Your veterinarian can advise you of the danger to your dog(s) in your area, and may suggest your dog be vaccinated for Lyme. Always go over your dog with a fine-toothed flea comb when you come in from walking through any area that may harbor deer ticks, and if your dog is acting unusually sluggish or sore, seek veterinary advice.

Attempts to pull a tick free will invariably leave the headpart in the pup, where it will die and cause an infected wound or abscess. The best way to remove ticks is to dab a strong saline solution on them, or iodine, or alcohol. This will numb them, causing them

Check your Pekingese's paws often. Seeds or thorns can get wedged in the fur or between his toes and cause a painful abscess.

Check your Peke's coat thoroughly for any fleas and ticks after he has been playing outside.

to loosen their hold, at which time they can be removed with forceps. The wound can then be cleaned and covered with an antiseptic ointment. If ticks are common in your area, consult with your vet for a suitable pesticide to be used in kennels, on bedding, and on the puppy or dog.

INSECTS AND OTHER OUTDOOR DANGERS

There are many biting insects, such as mosquitoes, that can cause discomfort to a puppy. Many diseases are transmitted by the males of these species. A pup can easily get a grass seed or thorn lodged between its pads or in the folds of its ears. These may go unnoticed until an abscess forms.

This is where your daily check of the puppy or dog will do a world of good. If your puppy has been playing in long grass or places where there may be thorns, pine needles, wild animals, or parasites, the check-up is a wise precaution.

SKIN DISORDERS

Apart from problems associated with lesions created by biting pests, a puppy may fall foul to a number of other skin disorders. Examples are ringworm, mange and eczema. Ringworm is not caused by a worm, but is a fungal infection. It manifests itself as a sore-looking bald circle. If your puppy should have any form of bald patches on himself, let your veterinarian check him over; a microscopic examination can confirm the condition. Many old remedies for ringworm exist, such as iodine, carbolic acid, formalin and other tinctures, but modern drugs are superior.

Fungal infections can be very difficult to treat, and even more difficult to eradicate, because of the spores. These can withstand most treatments, other than burning, which is the best thing to do with bedding once the condition has been confirmed.

Mange is a general term that can be applied to many skin conditions where the hair falls out and a flaky crust develops and falls away.

Often, dogs will scratch themselves, and this invariably is worse than the original condition, for it opens lesions that are then subject to viral, fungal or parasitic attack. The cause of the problem can be various species of mites. These either live on skin debris and the hair follicles, which they destroy, or they bury themselves just beneath the skin and feed on the tissue. Applying general remedies from pet stores is not recommended because it is essential to identify the type of mange before a specific treatment is effective.

Eczema is another non-specific term applied to many skin disorders. The condition can be brought about in many ways. Sunburn, chemicals, allergies to foods, drugs, pollens—even stress—can all produce a deterioration of the skin and coat. Given the range of causal factors, treatment can be difficult because the problem is one of identification. It is a case of taking each possibility at a time and trying to correctly diagnose the matter. If the cause is of a dietary nature, then you must remove one item at a time in order to find out if the dog is allergic to a given food. It could, of course, be the lack of a nutrient that is the problem, so if the condition persists, you should consult your veterinarian.

INTERNAL DISORDERS

It cannot be overstressed that it is very foolish to attempt to diagnose an internal disorder without the advice of a veterinarian. Take a relatively common problem such as diarrhea. It might be caused by nothing more serious than the puppy hogging a lot of food or eating something that it has never previously eaten. Conversely, it could be the first indication of a potentially fatal disease. It's up to your veterinarian to make the correct diagnosis.

The following symptoms, especially if they accompany each other or are progressively added to earlier symptoms, mean you should visit the veterinarian right away:

Continual vomiting. All dogs vomit from time to time and this is not necessarily a sign of illness. They will eat grass to induce vomiting. It is a natural cleansing process common to many carnivores. However, continued vomiting is a clear sign of a

Although this is typical behavior of an independent Peke, make an appointment with your vet if your Pekingese's behavior changes. For example, a loss of interest in food, prolonged listlessness, or crying when touched could indicate a health problem.

problem. It may be a blockage in the pup's intestinal tract, it may be induced by worms, or it could be due to any number of diseases.

Diarrhea. This, too, may be nothing more than a temporary condition due to many factors. Even a change of home can induce diarrhea, because this often stresses the pup, and invariably there is some change in the diet. If it persists more than 48 hours then something is amiss. If blood is seen in the feces, waste no time at all in taking the dog to the vet.

Running eyes and/or nose. A pup might have a chill and this will cause the eyes and noise to weep. Again, this should quickly clear up if the puppy is placed in a warm environment and away from any drafts. If it does not, and especially if a mucous discharge is seen, then the pup has an illness that must be diagnosed.

Coughing. Prolonged coughing is a sign of a problem, usually of a respiratory nature.

Wheezing. If the pup has difficulty breathing and makes a wheezing sound when breathing, then something is wrong.

Cries when attempting to defecate or urinate. This might only be a minor problem due to the hard state of the feces, but it could be more serious, especially if the pup cries when urinating.

Cries when touched. Obviously, if you do not handle a puppy with care he might yelp. However, if he cries even when lifted gently, then he has an internal problem which becomes apparent when pressure is applied to a given area of the body. Clearly, this must be diagnosed.

Refuses food. Generally, puppies and dogs are greedy creatures when it comes to feeding time. Some might be more fussy, but none should refuse more than

Roundworms are spaghetti-like worms that cause a pot-bellied appearance and dull coat, along with more sever symptoms, such as diarrhea and vomiting. Photo courtesy of Merck AgVet.

one meal. If they go for a number of hours without showing any interest in their food, then something is not as it should be.

General Listlessness. All puppies have their off days when they do not seem their usual cheeky, mischievous selves. If this condition persists for more than two days then there is little doubt of a problem. They may not show any of the signs listed, other than perhaps a reduced interest in their food. There are many diseases that can develop internally without displaying obvious clinical signs. Blood, fecal and other tests are needed in order to identify the disorder before it reaches and advanced state that may not be treatable.

WORMS

There are many species of worms, and a number of these live in the tissues of dogs and most other animals. Many create no problem at all, so you are not even aware they exist. Others can be tolerated in small levels, but become a major problem if they number more than a few. The most common types seen in dogs are roundworms and tapeworms. While roundworms are the greater problem, tapeworms require an intermediate host so are more easily eradicated.

Roundworms of the species *Toxocara canis* infest the dog. They may grow to a length of 8 inches (20 cm) and look like strings of spaghetti. The worms feed on the digesting food in the pup's intestines. In chronic cases the puppy will become pot-bellied, have diarrhea and will vomit. Eventually, he will stop eating, having passed through the stage when he always seems hungry. The worms lay eggs in the puppy and these pass out in his feces. They are then either ingested by the pup, or they are eaten by mice, rats or beetles. These may then be eaten by the puppy and the life cycle is complete.

Larval worms can migrate to the womb of a pregnant bitch, or to her mammary glands, and this is how they pass to the puppy. The pregnant bitch can be wormed, which will help. The pups can, and should, be wormed when they are about two weeks old. Repeat worming every 10 to 14 days and the parasites should be removed. Worms can be extremely dangerous to young puppies, so you should be sure the pup is wormed as a matter of routine.

Tapeworms can be seen as tiny rice-like eggs sticking to the puppy's or dog's anus. They are less destructive, but still undesirable. The eggs are eaten by mice, fleas, rabbits and other animals that serve as intermediate hosts. They develop into a larval stage and the host must be eaten by the dog in order to complete the chain. Your vet will supply a suitable remedy if tapeworms are seen or suspected. The vet can also do an egg count on the pup's feces under the microscope; this will indicate the extent of an infestation.

There are other worms, such as hookworms and whipworms, that are also blood suckers. They will make a pup anemic, and blood might be seen in the feces, which can be examined by the vet to confirm their presence. Cleanliness in all matters is the best preventative measure for all worms.

BLOAT (GASTRIC DILATATION)

This condition has proved fatal in many dogs, especially large and deep-chested breeds. However, any dog can get bloat. It is caused by gases building up in the stomach, especially in the small intestine. What happens is that carbohydrates are fermented and release gases. Normally, these gases are released by belching or by being passed from the anus. If for any reason these exits become blocked (such as if the stomach twists due to physical exertion), the gases cannot escape and the stomach simply swells and places pressure on other organs, sometimes cutting off the blood supply to the heart or causing suffocation. Death can easily follow if the condition goes undetected.

The best preventative measure is not to feed large meals or exercise your puppy or dog immediately after it has eaten. You can reduce the risk of flatulence by feeding more fiber in the diet, not feeding too many dry biscuits, and possibly by adding activated charcoal tablets to the diet.

ACCIDENTS

All puppies will get their share of bumps and bruises due to the rather energetic way they play. These will usually rectify themselves over a few days. Small cuts should be bathed with a suitable disinfectant and then smeared with an antiseptic ointment. If a cut looks more serious, then stem the flow of blood with a towel, or makeshift tourniquet and rush the pup to the veterinarian. Never apply so much pressure to the wound that it might restrict the flow of blood to the limb.

In the case of burns you should apply cold water or an ice pack to the surface. If the burn was due to a chemical then this must be washed away with copious amounts of water. Apply an antibiotic

Whipworms are hard to find unless you strain your dog's feces, and this is best left to a veterinarian. Pictured here are adult whipworms.

Keeping a watchful eye on your Pekingese will help prevent any accidents from happening.

ointment to the burn and, if necessary, wrap the dog in a blanket and rush him to the vet. The pup may go into shock, depending on the severity of the burn, and this will result in a lowered blood pressure, which is dangerous and the reason the pup must receive immediate veterinary attention.

If a broken limb is suspected then try to keep the animal as still as possible. Wrap your pup or dog in a blanket to restrict movement and get him to the veterinarian as soon as possible. Do not move the dog's head so it is tilting backward, as this might result in blood entering the lungs.

Do not let your pup jump up and down from heights, as this can cause considerable shock to the joints. Like all youngsters, puppies do not know when enough is enough, so you must do all their thinking for them.

Provided you apply strict hygiene to all aspects of your puppy's husbandry, and you make daily checks on his physical state, you have done as much as you can to safeguard him during his most vulnerable period. Routine visits to your veterinarian are also recommended, especially while the puppy is under one year of age. The vet may notice something that did not seem important to you.

Index

Photo Credits

Cammar, 48

Isabelle Francais, 1, 3, 4, 5, 7, 8, 9, 11, 16, 17, 18, 19(T), 20, 21, 22, 24, 25, 27, 28, 30, 31, 32(T), 34, 35, 36, 37, 38, 39, 40, 41, 42, 43, 44, 45, 46, 49, 50, 52, 53, 54, 56(B), 57

Barbara Gauthier, 14

Vernon Lorenzen, 19(B), 62

Tom and Linda Nutting, 15

DeAnn Ulmer, 13, 23, 26, 29, 32(B), 33, 47, 51, 59